Satellites

Experts on child reading levels
have consulted on the level of text and
concepts in this book.

At the end of the book is a "Look Back and Find" section
which provides additional information and encourages
the child to refer back to previous pages
for the answers to the questions posed.

Angela Grunsell trained as a teacher in 1969.
She has a Diploma in Reading and Related Skills
and for the last five years has advised London
teachers on materials and resources.
She works for the ILEA as an advisory teacher in
primary schools in Hackney, London.

Published in the United States in 1984 by
Franklin Watts, 387 Park Avenue South, New York, NY 10016

© Aladdin Books Ltd/Franklin Watts

Designed and produced by
Aladdin Books Ltd, 70 Old Compton Street, London W1

ISBN 0 531 04809 8

Library of Congress Catalog Card Number 84 50607

Printed in Belgium

FRANKLIN · WATTS · FIRST · LIBRARY

Satellites

by
Kate Petty

Consultant
Angela Grunsell

Illustrated by
Mike Saunders and Andrew Farmer

Franklin Watts
New York · London · Toronto · Sydney

Do you know what this is?

It is a satellite in orbit around the Earth.

That means it is circling the Earth in space.

There are about 300 of these satellites in orbit.

The Moon is a natural satellite of the Earth.
The satellites that we send into space
help us in many ways.

How does a satellite get into space?
Some are launched from the Earth by rockets.
The rocket fires in three stages. Each stage
sends the satellite further on its journey.

8

Some satellites can be launched in space.
First they are carried there in the cargo bay
of the Space Shuttle. A satellite must travel
at exactly the right speed to get into orbit.

Once the satellite is going around in orbit, it will stay there for many years. Small gas-fired jets drive it back on course if it drifts.

The little squares on the "wings" are solar panels. They make electricity from sunlight to power the instruments on board the satellite.

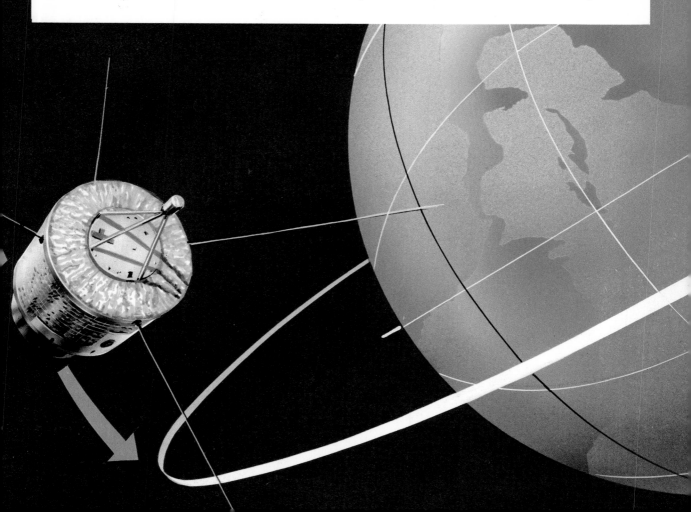

Although this satellite is in orbit, it seems to stay "fixed" in one spot high above the Earth. This is because it is going around 22,300 miles above the Equator at the same speed as the Earth spins.

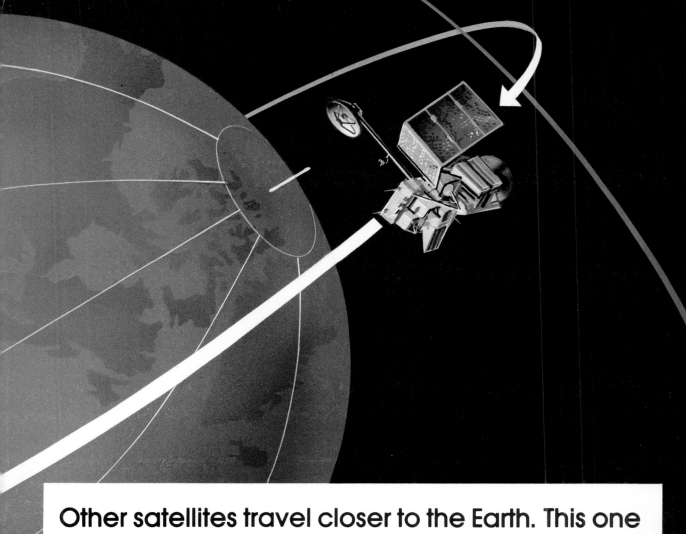

Other satellites travel closer to the Earth. This one goes around over the North Pole and South Pole in a "polar" orbit. As the Earth spins beneath its path it "sees" something different all the time.

Have you seen this view from a satellite before? It comes from a weather satellite in a polar orbit 560 miles above the ground.
It takes about 100 minutes to make one orbit of the Earth.

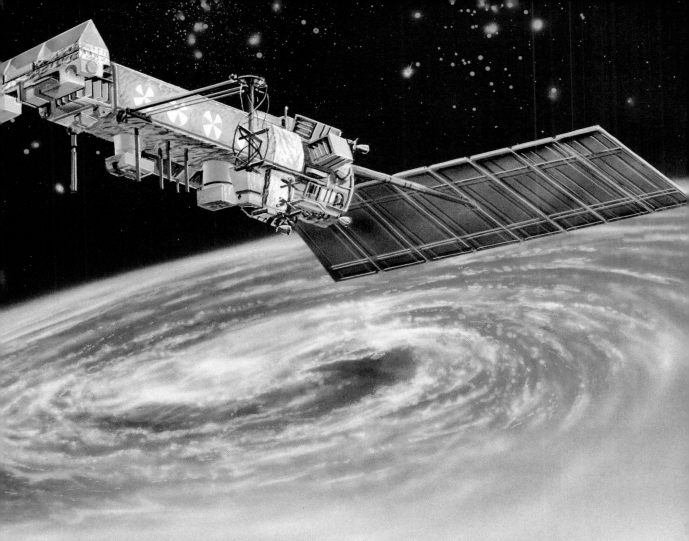

Here it is photographing a storm out at sea.
Five weather satellites, belonging to
different countries, stay in a "fixed" orbit.
Their early warnings of storms can save lives.

You can follow a tennis match on TV even though it is happening on the other side of the world. Can you see how the TV signals are "bounced" off the satellite from one continent to another?

The satellite is called a Comsat.
It is also used for relaying international
phone calls. Comsat can take up to 12,000
phone calls at a time.

Can you think how ships might use satellites? They can find out their position at sea using signals from several "fixed" satellites. They can pick up weather information from them too.

Satellites can help a ship – or a plane –
in an emergency by relaying distress signals
straight to the rescue station.

Pictures sent back from satellites are used
for making maps. Not all of them are ordinary
photographs. This infrared picture can show
where crops grow and how healthy they are.

Radar pictures can show where water is.
This satellite picture shows where
it has been raining.

What happens when a satellite breaks down in space? It could be picked up by the Space Shuttle and repaired by astronauts.

Satellite "Solar Max" had a power failure.
The astronauts were able to mend it.
It was soon launched into orbit again.

This satellite is an observatory, sending back information about distant stars. It picks up rays that can't pass through the Earth's atmosphere.

The Space Telescope will be launched in 1985. From its position high above Earth's atmosphere it will "see" deeper into space than anything before it.

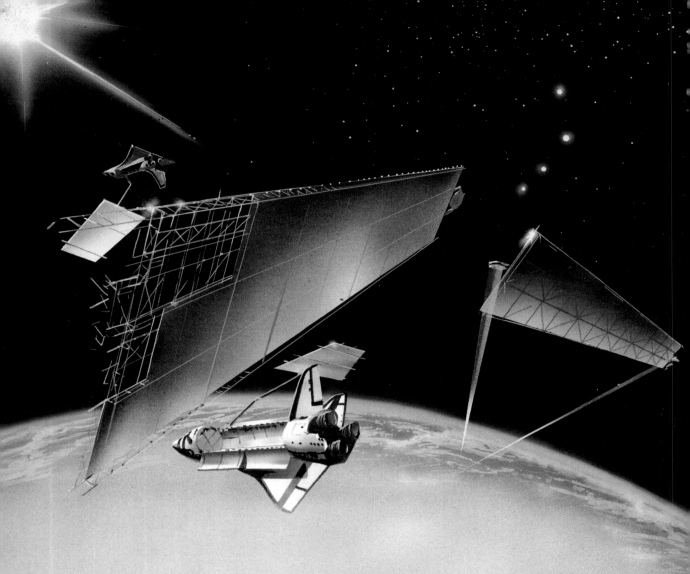

These are giant power satellites of the future.
Their solar panels would beam down energy
from the Sun for us to use on Earth.

You have seen how useful satellites
are already in your everyday life.
They belong to a space age
which is only just beginning.

Look back and find

How does this rocket take a satellite into space?

How are other satellites launched?

How fast must a satellite travel to get into orbit?
At a speed of 17,400 mph.

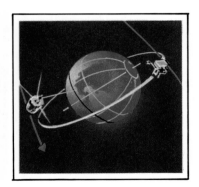

How long does a satellite in a "fixed" orbit take to go around the Earth?
24 hours — the same time it takes the Earth to spin around once.

What is the Equator?
An imaginary line dividing the Northern half from the Southern half of the world.

Do you know why this satellite is called Comsat?
Comsat is short for communications satellite.

What is this satellite used for?

Why are satellites useful to ships?

How do the rescue services know the ship is in distress?

Can you see satellites from Earth?
Yes, on a clear night you might see winking lights moving across the sky.

What is the astronaut doing in this picture?

How long does a satellite stay in orbit?
Satellites which are high above the Earth might stay in orbit for 100 or 1,000 years. Nearer satellites might come down after 5 years, burning up as they meet Earth's atmosphere.

What is this satellite called?
HEOS – which stands for High Energy Observatory Satellite.

Why can a telescope in space get a better view of the stars than one on the ground?

Index

PRINTED IN BELGIUM BY

proost
INTERNATIONAL BOOK PRODUCTION